Dale Earnhardt, Jr.
A Car Racer Who Cares

Ken Rappoport

Enslow Elementary

an imprint of

Enslow Publishers, Inc.

40 Industrial Road
Box 398
Berkeley Heights, NJ 07922
USA

http://www.enslow.com

Enslow Elementary, an imprint of Enslow Publishers, Inc.

Enslow Elementary® is a registered trademark of Enslow Publishers, Inc.

Library of Congress Cataloging-in-Publication Data

Rappoport, Ken.
  Dale Earnhardt, Jr. : a car racer who cares / Ken Rappoport.
     p. cm.—(Sports stars who care)
     Includes bibliographical references and index.
     Summary: "A biography of race car driver Dale Earnhardt, Jr.,
  highlighting his charitable work"—Provided by publisher.
     ISBN 978-0-7660-3777-9
     1. Earnhardt, Dale, Jr.—Juvenile literature. 2. Stock car drivers—United States
  —Biography—Juvenile literature. 3. Philanthropists—United States—Biography—
  Juvenile literature. I. Title.
     GV1032.E19R37 2011
     796.72092—dc22
     [B]
                                2010014947

122010 Lake Book Manufacturing, Inc., Melrose Park, IL

Printed in the United States of America

10 9 8 7 6 5 4 3 2 1

To Our Readers:
We have done our best to make sure all Internet addresses in this book were active and appropriate
when we went to press. However, the author and the publisher have no control over and assume
no liability for the material available on those Internet sites or on other Web sites they may link to.
Any comments or suggestions can be sent by e-mail to comments@enslow.com or to the address on
the back cover.

Illustration Credits: AP/Wide World Photos, pp. 1, 6, 9, 10, 13, 15, 19, 21, 24, 26, 27, 29, 32, 34,
36, 37, 39, 40, 42, 43; Ida Mae Astute/© American Broadcasting Companies, Inc./courtesy Everett
Collection, p. 4; Russell Labounty/CSM/Landov, p. 41.

Cover Illustration: AP/Wide World Photos (Earnhardt holding up Talladega trophy)

Contents

Dale Earnhardt, Jr., was born to race. Both his father and grandfather were famous race car drivers.

Introduction

Dale Earnhardt, Jr., is the son of one of the most famous race car drivers in NASCAR history.

Not many could compare to Dale Earnhardt, Sr. He set high levels with seven Cup titles and seventy-six tour victories in a fast-paced career.

Dale Jr.'s grandfather created his own records at the racetrack.

Young Dale had a lot to live up to in the sport. What did he do? He won two titles in the Busch series for beginning drivers.

Then he claimed success over veteran drivers in the top level Cup series.

Here is the story of Dale Earnhardt, Jr. He became one of the most popular and successful drivers in stock-car racing.

Dale Earnhardt, Sr., hoists up the trophy for winning the NASCAR Cracker Barrel 500 race.

It was the summer of 2001. Dale Earnhardt, Jr., was getting ready for the most important race of his life. Just five months earlier his famous father, Dale Earnhardt, Sr., died in a car crash. It happened at the Daytona International Speedway.

Chapter 1

Remembering Dad

Dale had not only lost a father, but a friend and coach. Dale loved racing because his father loved racing. Dale would often ask his father for help. Now, for the first time, he would be racing without him. Now he was all alone.

Everyone was counting on him to win races. He wanted to be a star like his father. *Could he do it? Could he be a star?*

Dale, Sr., had won Rookie of the Year honors in 1979. He went on to win seven Cups as racing's stock-car champion. That matched Richard Petty's record.

NASCAR champions are rated by a points system. It is based on their racing record during the year. The 1987 season was Dale, Sr.'s best: 11 victories and 24 finishes in the top 10 in just 29 races.

The Earnhardt family was born to race. Dale's grandfather, Ralph Earnhardt, was a star in the racing world from the 1950s to the 1970s.

Dale, Jr., was keeping the family tradition alive. He did it in a different style than his roughhouse dad.

Dale, Sr., was nicknamed the Intimidator. He roared around the track in his black car. He was fearless. He did not care if he caused a car to crash. His "bad boy" image followed him. Dale, Sr., had

Dale Earnhardt, Jr.'s grandfather, Ralph Earnhardt, drove car #75. He started to spin out during the Rebel 300 race, which took place May 14, 1962.

few friends on the track. Unlike his father, Dale, Jr., is very popular among his fellow drivers.

Since his father helped him to get started, Dale, Jr., has been a fast learner. He only needed twelve starts to win a Winston Cup race.

Dale Earnhardt, Sr., (#3) sped ahead of Mike Skinner (#31) and Dale Earnhardt, Jr., (#8) to win the Winston 500 on October 15, 2000. Father and son have had to race against each other many times, but they always supported each other.

Now it was 2001. Earnhardt was at Daytona—the same track that took his father's life.

The Daytona track is one of the major stops in the stock-car racing world. The huge oval hosts as many as 180,000 fans. It had featured stock-car racing's stars. These included Petty, Bobby Allison, David Pearson, Darrell Waltrip, and, of course, Dale Earnhardt, Sr.

The major race at the Daytona track is the Daytona 500. It is NASCAR's biggest race. Some call it the "Great American Race." In 1998, Dale, Sr., had won the Daytona 500.

And now Dale, Jr., was racing in the Pepsi 400 not long after his father's death.

Earnhardt settled into his car. He looked down the steeply banked, 2.5-mile track. He knew there would be 400 miles of hard driving ahead of him, 160 spins around the track in all.

Growing up, Dale never thought he would be here.

Go, Dodge Charger, go!

Dale, Jr., was very young when he played with Matchbox cars. Lining them up, he pretended he was racing. He made sure he always won.

Chapter 2

Growing Up Earnhardt

Dale, Sr., won the Busch Clash Stock Car Race on February 9, 1986. Junior was eleven years old at the time.

But a little thought was always there: *You can never be as good as your dad.*

"As a kid, I'd look at my daddy and look at how [tough] he was," Dale, Jr., said.

Everyone in his household was excited about racing and race cars. Family cars came last.

"For our family cars we drove old junk Chevelles—anything you could get for $200," Dale's dad said.

Dale, Jr., loved going to his father's car shop. He went only when asked. Those were his father's rules.

"The night before, you would hang out with him while he watched television, just hoping he might say something," Dale, Jr., said.

When Dale was allowed to go, he was thrilled. There was nothing better than standing next to a race car.

Dale never dreamed he would some day be driving against the world's best race car drivers.

He was 4 feet 10 inches tall as a freshman in high school. As a shy teenager, Dale wondered,

Dale Earnhardt, Jr., won his second Busch Series title on September 10, 1999.

"How am I going to become some [tough] race car driver?"

He saw himself as a mechanic. He enjoyed working around cars. Nobody could change oil as fast as the teenage Dale at his father's auto shop.

Dale, Jr., was born on October 10, 1974, in Kannapolis, North Carolina. His birth name: Ralph Dale Earnhardt, Jr. He was named after both his grandfather and father. Dale had more than one nickname. He was called "Little E," "Junebug," or "Junior."

Dale, Jr., looked up to his father, grandfather, older sister, Kelley, and older brother, Kerry. All of them drove race cars. Dale helped his sister and brother by working on their cars. Then he started thinking about being a race car driver. Dale worked on his own car. At the age of seventeen, he was competing on the track.

DID YOU KNOW?

Dale, Jr., and Kerry made $300 selling a go-cart, which they used to buy a car to rebuild and race.

"Working on your own car came last with my dad because that was a privilege," Dale, Jr., said. "I helped Kelley on Friday, and I raced my car on Saturday."

Five years after he started working on his own race car, Dale, Jr., was a pro.

It was 1995 when he entered his first Busch Series race. He finished fourteenth.

He moved up quickly. He finished as high as second in 1997. By 1998, Dale, Jr., was invited to drive full-time for his father's racing team. He started fast. He won the Busch Series title that year. Then he won his second in 1999.

Next stop: the Winston Cup series. How would Dale do against the top pro racers in the world?

Welcome to the big time, Dale, Jr. Eleven races. No wins. The Winston Cup series was proving to be a challenge. Now it was the summer of 2000. Dale was entered in the DirecTV 500 at the Texas Motor Speedway.

Chapter 3

Victory Lane

It was a family affair. Dale would be racing against his own father.

His father did everything he could to help his son prepare for the race. Dale's father made sure Dale had the best of everything. He put together a talented driving team. He chose the powerful Chevy car Dale would drive.

Dale Earnhardt, Jr., (#8) passes his father (#3) in the Coca-Cola 600 on May 28, 2000.

It was time for the race. Dale waited eagerly in his car for the signal to start.

The air filled with the thunder of powerful engines exploding in ear-splitting noise.

Then . . . they are off!

Dale, Jr., took the lead.

"I didn't have to do a whole lot," he said.

The car was so good it did not need any changes during the race.

"I'd just point and shoot, and that thing ran." Dale, Jr., said. "It was easy as pie to drive."

Earnhardt, Jr., quickly moved in front at the 1.5-mile track in Fort Worth, Texas. Caution flags slowed him down. They stopped him from building his lead.

The last thirty-nine laps were run under green flags. It meant the track was clear.

Dale, Jr., built a bigger lead in that stretch. He finished ahead of the field by a 5.920-second margin. Dale, Jr., did it without using the dangerous driving methods of his father. In all, he led for a race-best 106 of 334 laps.

Dale Earnhardt, Sr., proudly hugs his son after Dale, Jr., won the Winston All-Star race on May 20, 2000.

DID YOU KNOW?

Junior's first start in the top minor league of racing was at the Carolina Pride 250.

Dale, Jr., let out a loud whoop as he crossed the finish line. It was party time in Victory Lane. His first Winston Cup victory was in the books!

Earnhardt, Sr., finished seventh in the field, but did not mind too much. After all, he had the pleasure of seeing his son finish first. "He was pretty excited," Dale, Jr., said.

Earnhardt, Jr., had a terrific crew to thank, and most importantly, his famous father.

One year later, Dale Earnhardt, Jr., would face the greatest tragedy of his life.

The newspaper headlines told the tragic story:

DALE EARNHARDT, SR., KILLED IN CRASH AT DAYTONA

The death of Dale's father on February 18, 2001 sent

Chapter 4

Family Tragedy

shock waves around the racing world. It sent Dale, Jr., into a tailspin.

In the wake of his father's death, Junior had dropped in the point standings for the Winston Cup. NASCAR had lost its most familiar face. Earnhardt had lost a father and main supporter.

Dale Earnhardt, Sr., (right) and Ken Schrader race side-by-side in the Daytona 500 on February 18, 2001, minutes before they crash. Earnhardt died in the accident.

Others in the racing crew had felt the blow, too.

"Dale was like a dad to me and to several other people on the team," said Earnhardt's car chief.

As a driver in the race, Dale, Jr., had seen the accident. He finished just after his father had crashed on the last lap.

The memory of the crash had stayed with him. Five months later, he was facing the most important race of his life. He wanted to win it for his dad.

The question: Could he carry on in his father's footsteps? Could he be a star?

The race: the Pepsi 400.

The track: Daytona.

Hard to believe—this was the same track that had taken his father's life.

The accident had cast a shadow over the first half of the 2001 racing season. NASCAR started to check safety for drivers. There was a report his father's belt had broken in the crash.

Fans hold up three fingers during the third lap of the Pepsi 400 race July 7, 2001, in memory of Dale Earnhardt, Sr., who drove car No. 3. He was killed on that same track, the Daytona International Speedway, only five months earlier.

All of this was on Junior's mind as he prepared for his first race since losing his father.

Dale quickly moved out in front in the Pepsi 400. His car led for 108 of the first 145 laps.

"We were just racing for second," said one of the drivers.

Dale Earnhardt, Jr., zooms across the finish line, winning the Pepsi 400 in honor of his father.

With 17 laps left, a twelve-car crash slowed down the race. It allowed several cars to catch up. Suddenly, Earnhardt found himself in seventh place. His crew chief felt all was lost. He did not think there was enough time to regain the lead. Earnhardt did not give up. It was too important.

He found an opening on the same strip of roadway where his father had crashed. Earnhardt hit the pedal.

He needed only two laps to take the lead. This time, he kept it. He won the most emotional race of his life.

Dale, Earnhardt, Jr., pulled his Chevy onto the infield grass. He spun the car around with several "donut" slides. His father had done slides after winning the Daytona 500 for the first time in 1998. Then Earnhardt jumped on the roof of the car. There were hugs and high-fives all around.

"Shoot, I don't really care what happens after this," Earnhardt said. "It doesn't get any better than this."

Dale Earnhardt, Jr., defeats Tony Stewart in the 2004 Daytona 500.

In 2004, Dale Earnhardt, Jr., won the "Great American Race" at the Daytona 500. The senior Earnhardt had won the very same race six years earlier.

DID YOU KNOW?

Dale, Sr., won thirty-four races at Daytona International Speedway, but did not win the Daytona 500 until 1998.

"Every time we come to Daytona, it feels like I'm closer to Dad," Dale said. "But at the same time, it's a reminder of losing him. So I wanted to come down here and win."

Later that year, a practice session was about to turn deadly.

ale Earnhardt's Corvette crashed and burst into flames.

A practice session for a race had turned Earnhardt's car into a fiery death trap. It happened in Sonoma, California, in the summer of 2004.

Chapter 5

A Crash and the Road Back

Earnhardt tried to free himself. The flames and heat became intense.

"The heat got up to more than 1,000 degrees," Earnhardt said. "I was in the car for 14 seconds."

In those fourteen seconds, he suffered burns on his neck, legs, and face.

"The pain was intense," he said.

Dale Earnhardt, Jr., drives his yellow Corvette just before he crashes and his car catches fire during warm-up practice on July 18, 2004.

The road back to the track would be just as painful. Dale's mother, Brenda Jackson, moved into his home. She became his nurse.

Imagine returning to the track just one week after the accident. That is just what Dale did.

On July 25, 2004, he raced in the Siemens 300 at the New Hampshire Speedway. Doctors advised him not to drive the entire race.

Earnhardt carefully climbed into his Chevy. It was a difficult and painful ride. He was not going to let his team down. But the pain forced him to stop after sixty-one laps.

His crew pulled him through the driver's window. He was covered with sweat and felt weak. But he made it. He held on to second place in the Cup standings.

Dale said the ride was like "getting burned all over again."

The next time was better. On August 28, Dale won the Sharpie 500 at Bristol, Tennessee.

Next stop: Talladega.

Dale walked away from his accident with second-degree burns to his body. He was in pain, but at least he was alive.

The super speedway was one of Earnhardt's favorite tracks. The Alabama oval was the largest (2.66 miles long) with very steep sides.

In his last six starts at Talladega, Dale had won four times. He was a big fan favorite there.

"It's gotten so crazy that I can't walk around the infield at Talladega without causing an uproar," Dale said. "But I like this place. It's been good to me."

Earnhardt was not hard to spot from the stands. He drove a bright red car with the number eight painted on its side. Many in the noisy crowd of 150,000 were dressed in red to support their favorite driver.

Dale stayed at or near the front for most of the race. That is, until his crew chief called him in for a pit stop. The chief wanted to change the tires on the right side of the car.

It was a big gamble. While Dale pulled in for the stop, other cars moved in front of him. By the time he got back on the track, he found himself in eleventh place. There were only five laps to go.

Crew members pull Dale out of his car on the fifty-third lap of the Pennsylvania 500 August 1, 2004. He was still recovering from the July 18 crash, but his injuries did not stop him from doing what he loved—racing.

Dale wasted no time in making up ground. The tire change worked. With the new tires, he moved quickly through the field. He finally took over the lead for good.

Winner: Dale Earnhardt, Jr., by two car lengths!

Dale's car is in the lead on the last lap of the EA Sports 500 at the Talladega Superspeedway October 3, 2004.

"Those brand-new rights just drove around the corners so much better than those other guys with old tires out there," Earnhardt said.

Dale's fifth win of the season raised him into first place in the overall point standings. The fiery crash that almost took his life was now forgotten in the moment of victory.

Three years later, Dale Jr.'s racing career would take a sharp turn.

Dale, Jr., was scared.

He had made the hardest decision of his life.

"Man, am I doing the right thing?" he wondered aloud.

He was leaving the team that his father had built.

Chapter 6

A New Direction

October 3, 2004

WINNER

Dale, Jr., won the EA Sports 500 at Talladega in 2004.

It was 2007. Until now, his whole life had been connected to racing and his father's company, Dale Earnhardt Incorporated (DEI).

Dale, Jr., was thirty-two years old. He had 40 pro race victories. He had more than two hundred Top 10 finishes, all of them with DEI.

Since his father's death, his stepmother, Teresa Earnhardt, had taken over DEI. Growing up, Dale, Jr., was never close to her.

Earnhardt shows off his car's new paint job in celebration of Hendrick Motorsports twenty-fifth anniversary at the Daytona International Speedway. Dale, Jr., signed up with Hendrick after his contract with his father's company, Dale Earnhardt Inc., ended.

Dale Earnhardt, Jr., (middle) poses with kids from the Boys and Girls Club of Bristol, Tennessee, August 24, 2007. Dale, along with Howard Heckes, the president of the Sharpie company, helped hand out backpacks for the Speedway Children's Charity.

When Dale, Jr., was younger, his father and Teresa were on the road a lot. The Earnhardt kids were under the care of relatives and others. During that time, Dale, Jr., got into a lot of trouble. He was kicked out of private school for fighting. He was sent to military school. He hated it and blamed his stepmother.

"It sure [. . .] wasn't my decision," Dale said. "It wasn't fun, I'll tell you that."

Dale and his stepmother could not agree on his new contract. It ended after the 2007 season.

Earnhardt, Jr., decided to drive for Hendrick Motorsports in 2008. Rick Hendrick had been a close friend of his father. As a teenager, Dale worked at the race track. One day, the friendly owner of Hendrick Motorsports called him over.

Jamie McMurray won the Daytona 500 on February 14, 2010, with Dale Earnhardt, Jr., coming in second place. Dale may have lost the race, but he never stopped believing in himself.

He drew up a make-believe contract on a paper napkin. Dale scribbled his name, all in good fun.

Now it had really come true. Dale was looking forward to being with a racing team where he felt like family. Dale, Jr.'s stepmother was never there when Dale won his races.

"I want a guy who's going to be at the track and give me feedback. I want to feel really part of an entire organization.

Dale Earnhardt, Jr., climbs into his car May 15, 2010, during practice for the Sprint Cup Series Autism Speaks 400 race taking place the next day.

That's a big part of racing, and I want that," Dale said.

Hendrick gave bear hugs to his winning drivers. It was clear he thought of his team as a giant family.

In December 2009, Dale, Jr., was also getting feedback from his fans. For the seventh straight year, he won the title of NASCAR's most popular driver.

Only two drivers had won more. They were Bill Elliott (16) and Richard Petty (9).

Dale was popular for his racing skills and his charity work. He has started the Dale, Jr., Foundation to help kids in need.

After signing with the Hendrick group, Dale went through a tough period on the track. He did not lose confidence in himself.

He had been through tough times before and came out on top. Just like his father, he would never back down. Nothing would stop him from carrying on.

His father had taught him well.

Career Statistics

SEASON	RACES	WINS	POLES	TOP 10S	EARNINGS	FINAL RANK
1999	5	0	0	1	$162,095	48
2000	34	2	2	5	$2,583,475	16
2001	36	3	2	15	$5,384,627	8
2002	36	2	2	16	$4,564,976	11
2003	36	2	0	21	$4,868,871	3
2004	36	6	0	21	$7,121,380	3
2005	36	1	0	13	$5,758,332	19
2006	36	1	0	17	$7,108,18	6
2007	36	0	1	12	$5,114,155	16
2008	36	1	1	17	$4,491,765	12
2009	36	0	0	5	$4,093,114	25

Where to Write

DALE EARNHARDT, JR.
c/o The Dale Jr. Foundation
P.O. Box 330
Mooresville, NC 28115

cockpit—Where the driver sits.

infield—The enclosed area on race tracks that includes team garages, drivers' trailers, and motor homes.

NASCAR—The National Association for Stock Car Auto Racing, which controls the major stock-car races in America.

Nationwide Series—One level down from the Sprint Cup. It is formerly know as the Busch series.

pit—A space for one car along pit row.

pit row—A traffic lane set aside off the track where pits for all the cars in a race are lined up end to end. Also called pit road.

pit stops—The times during a race when a race car stops in its pit for the racing crew to quickly change tires and refuel.

Sprint Cup Series—The highest level of stock-car racing. It is formerly known as the Winston Cup and the Nextel Cup. The champion is decided by a driver's point total based on his finishes in the season's races.

stock cars—Race cars that are made to look like and have the same names as ordinary cars on the road. The names are Chevrolet, Dodge, Ford, and Toyota.

super speedway—An oval track that is at least one mile long. The major tracks are often more than two miles in length.

throttle—The gas pedal.

Books

Caldwell, Dave. *Speed Show: How NASCAR Won The Heart of America*. Boston, Mass.: Kingfisher, 2006.

Ford, Michael. *Dale Earnhardt Jr.* Milwaukee: Gareth Stevens, 2010.

Savage, Jeff. *Dale Earnhardt Jr.* Minneapolis: First Avenue Editions, 2009.

Internet Addresses

Dale Earnhardt, Jr. Official Site
http://www.dalejr.com

Jr.'s Fan Site
http://www.jr-nation.com/dale_jr/

The Dale Jr. Foundation
http://www.thedalejrfoundation.org